Bright Ideas for Early Years

Getting Started

Linda Mort & Janet Morris

Published by Scholastic Publications Ltd,
Marlborough House, Holly Walk,
Leamington Spa, Warwickshire,
CV32 4LS.

©1989 Scholastic Publications Ltd

Written by Linda Mort and Janet Morris
Edited by Jackie Cunningham-Craig
Sub-edited by Jane Morgan
Designed by Sue Limb
Illustrations by Jane Bottomley

Artwork by Liz Preece, Castle Graphics,
Kenilworth.
Printed in Great Britain by
Loxley Brothers Ltd, Sheffield

British Library Cataloguing in Publication Data
Mort, Linda
  Getting started. – (Bright ideas for early years)
  1. Nursery Schools. Teaching
  I. Title II. Morris, Janet III. Series
  372.11'02

  ISBN 0-590-76152-8

Front and back cover: designed by
Sue Limb
Photographs by Martyn Chillmaid
and Sue Limb.

Contents

For Andrew, David,
Leonie and Alexander.

Introduction

Getting Started has been written specially for anyone working with three to six-year-olds, whether in playgroups, day nurseries, family centres, nursery schools, nursery classes or reception classes. *Getting Started* aims to give children a successful start to pre-school and school life, and to introduce the groundwork necessary for the adults involved in such areas as organising the physical environment, settling in new children and involving parents.

This book draws upon recent research findings into young children's learning which emphasise the importance of arranging the surroundings so that children become independent initiators of their own learning, developing the vital life skills necessary for a rapidly changing world. Children can no longer be the passive recipients of knowledge dispensed by adults. Appropriate opportunities for self-motivated learning can be facilitated by adults, through careful observation of children's play and sensitive interaction with them through conversation.

Play is seen as the most important learning medium for both the pre-school and the reception child. The role of the adult in structuring the play is explored in practical terms, including talking with children as they play, in order to bring out the maximum learning potential in a supportive but non-directive way. Play is the child's work and adults must be involved – children should no longer be left to play by themselves in order to allow the adults to concentrate on 'doing work' with others.

Setting up

The chapter on Setting up concentrates on how recent research findings can be translated into the practical terms of arranging the large items of furniture and storage facilities in a 'self-service' room into 'interest areas'. In such learning workshops, everything is visible and accessible to the children so they can easily find and replace everything they need and so develop independent decision-making and problem-solving skills and attitudes.

The self-service room

The self-service room chapter describes the kind of resources that can be placed in each interest area of the self-service room, and the role of adults in interacting with the children in their use of the resources, in order to support and develop the learning experiences. The chapter includes ideas on talking with children as they play, so that planning, thinking and communication skills are developed, which is a firm foundation for the kind of learning emphasised in the National Curriculum.

Settling in

The chapter on settling in deals with settling new children into pre-school and reception classes. There is special emphasis on the needs of four-year-olds

in reception classes. This chapter takes into account the fact that although nursery standards of staffing should apply in the reception class, there will be many situations in which this will not be the case. Ideas are included for the provision of challenging outdoor play, a vital need which cannot be adequately met without sufficient staffing and appropriate financial resources.

Keeping in touch

Keeping in touch is concerned with parental involvement and includes ideas on how communication with parents can be a two-way process.

About this book

The material is applicable to both pre-school and reception settings. Where ideas are offered as being more suitable to the pre-school stage, the letter (P) is used. Similarly the letter (R) is used for ideas which are mainly appropriate to the reception class. The letter (M) is used for pre-school settings, such as playgroups, where the furniture and storage facilities have to be movable to enable everything to be put away on a regular basis.

Throughout the book boys and girls have been referred to indiscriminately in an attempt to avoid a stereotyped attitude in what they are encouraged to do.

7

Setting up

Chapter one

The '5Cs'

- Choice
- Concentration
- Creativity
- Co-operation
- Communication

The main findings of recent research into young children's learning all point to the importance of organising an environment which maximises the opportunities for self-motivated, creative learning.

Playgroups, nurseries and reception classes which are planned to enable children to learn in this way, will be laying firm foundations for all future learning, in a manner which is the most appropriate to young children's needs. The vital, independent, problem-solving, communicative learning emphasised in the National Curriculum has its origins in an early years curriculum based on the importance of learning through play and language development.

Young children should be helped to make meaningful choices about their activities right from the start, and be encouraged to plan these decisions, talk about them with adults and other children, and carry them through. Children who are allowed to choose their own activities will tend, with adult support, to concentrate well. The value of allowing children to concentrate without interruption for long periods in self-chosen tasks, has been shown to be an important factor in intellectual development. Adults should provide opportunities for children to engage in creative, challenging play in which a wide variety of different materials can be combined and transformed. This will provide opportunities to develop problem-solving skills and attitudes.

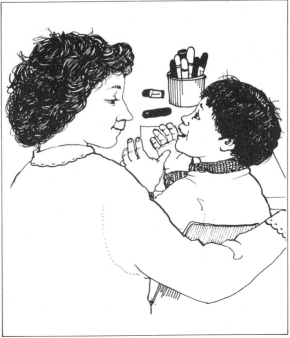

Children should be encouraged to co-operate with others, especially in pairs and small groups, and be given the chance to communicate their questions and discoveries to each other and to adults. Adults should not feel inhibited about actively involving themselves in children's play. The participating adult has the ability, through conversation, to support and extend the play and bring out the maximum learning potential.

The self-service room

In order for young children to make choices and plan their activities, it is necessary that they can see what is available, and be able to find what they need by themselves, without being dependent on adults. For this reason, playgroups, nurseries and reception classes should be organised along self-service principles. The self-service room is best organised into interest areas:

- The getting together area.
- The theme area (for fantasy and role-play). For children's purposes, you may wish to call this the 'Dressing-up Corner' or whatever the area happens to be at the time (eg an airport). It should not be exclusively a home corner all the time (see page 37).
- The creative floor play space.
- The library.
- The listening corner.
- The drawing and pre-writing area (P) or the writing area (R).
- The quiet area (for table construction games, mosaics, jigsaws, puzzles, threading, sewing etc).
- The maths area (R).
- The art area.
- The discovery area (including sand and water).
- The outdoor play area.

Each interest area should contain all the necessary resources related to that area, easily available to the children and colour-coded for speedy tidying up.

A room organised into interest areas, where the children can clearly understand the different learning opportunities and are able to see what is available, will facilitate their decision-making and planning skills and their ability to make independent choices. Children will no longer need to ask, 'What shall I do now?'.

In 'movable' rooms, such as playgroups, where everything has to be put away at the end of the day or week, it is equally possible and beneficial to arrange the room in interest areas.

Knowing the exact layout of the room and where everything is kept gives children the security and confidence to plan their decisions in advance. Children just starting playgroup or nursery can be gradually introduced to the idea of planning their activity. Over a period of time, children will steadily, with guidance, and as much conversation as possible with adults and other children, come to take responsibility for their own learning. They will concentrate for increasingly longer periods without the necessity for frequent clearing up. Because a wide range of play materials is constantly available to be combined in creative ways, the room becomes a stimulating and challenging environment, in which children are naturally motivated to talk about, and ask questions about, their discoveries. The interest areas are genuinely interesting to the children.

Children's creativity and imagination are not dependent and limited by what adults have 'put out' for them, and opportunities for uninterrupted pair and small group work, are enhanced. Adults have much greater opportunity to observe the children in their choice of activities and to talk with them at length, helping them to think out their ideas beforehand, extend the possibilities of the plan in terms of the child's individual learning, and to discuss it afterwards, than they would

have in a more traditional set-up. This is because they are largely freed from routine matters of classroom management such as 'giving things out' and maintaining order.

In self-service environments, the amount of time spent waiting for the teacher's attention can be almost entirely eliminated. This is especially important in reception classes, where there can be only one teacher in charge of many four-year-olds. It is possible to plan a room or rooms based on interest areas for every kind of situation in which young children learn, for playgroups with 'movable' or permanent furniture and equipment, for nursery schools and classes, and for reception classes. The main principles involved apply equally to all pre-school and reception settings.

Planning the room

What you need
White paper, coloured paper, room measurements, scissors.

What to do
Make an approximate plan of the room on white paper. Decide on a different colour for each interest area, then cut out proportionately sized and shaped pieces of coloured paper to represent each area. These can be moved on the white paper as you decide on the best layout. Some suggestions to bear in mind are:

- Making the theme area at least one fifth the size of the room, if possible.
- Positioning the creative floor play space next to the theme area, so that children's constructions (eg boats, planes etc) can be incorporated into the play of the theme area.
- Siting the library on the other side of the theme area so that children will be encouraged to make an immediate link between the world of books and the world of fantasy and role-play.
- The getting together area should be large enough for the whole group to sit together, often in a circle. A good position is in the middle of the room where all the children can be called together quickly. If, however, space is limited, the getting together area can double up as the creative floor play area.
- The art area should share a tiled floor with the sand and water, preferably near to a sink.

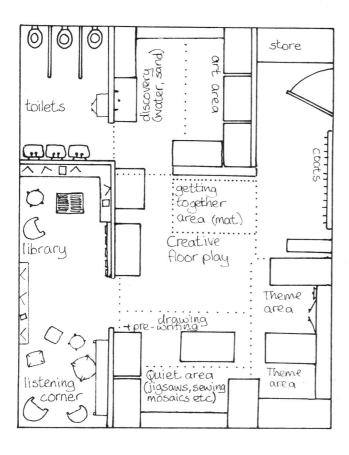

Posters

What you need

Coloured sugar paper; white paper or card; pictures cut from magazines, educational supplies catalogues or hand drawn; camera (optional); adhesive; felt-tipped pen; hole punch (M); string (M); suction towel hooks (M).

What to do

Make large colourful posters (about 60 cm x 40 cm) to 'advertise' each interest area. Each poster should have a different-coloured background to correspond with your room plan. The posters can be purely visual, showing children engaged in the activity of the interest area. It is especially valuable if you can find pictures of equipment, construction toys etc which are used by children. If preferred, you may wish to photograph the children in each interest area, and use these instead.

You can add print, in the form of speech bubbles, questions or slogans. These posters can be a valuable language resource to help the children plan what they want to do.

In movable rooms, where posters cannot be left permanently on walls, attach string to each poster and hang up using rubber suction towel hooks.

14

Language in action

What you need
Coloured card and/or old free-standing photograph frames (minus glass), felt-tipped pens.

What to do
Using simple pictures, symbols, signs, arrows, cartoons and captions taken from real examples of environmental print, make notices to help the children organise themselves. Ask the children for their ideas about signs needed on surfaces next to displays etc. They can be put inside old photograph frames.

The getting together area

What you need
A space large enough for the whole group to sit together (often in a circle); a carpet or blanket(s) (M); chair(s) for adult(s); a notice-board (eg child-sized easel); a display table, or set of shelves or 3-tier trolley.

What to do
The notice-board can be fixed to the back of the display table or mounted on a small movable easel. As well as using this area for stories, songs, music and games, it can also be used for listening to children's planning and recalling of their experiences.

Corners, areas and bays

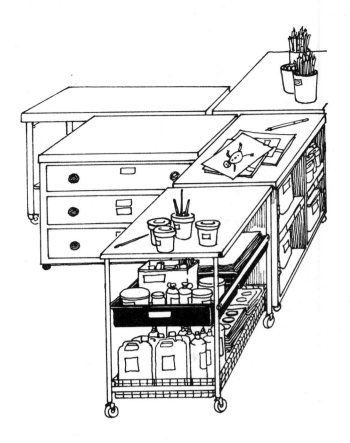

What you need

Low cupboards, low drawer units, rectangular tables, bookshelves, tea trolleys, plastic storage baskets, ice-cream cartons, sugar paper, card, magazine and catalogue pictures, felt-tipped pens, covering film, sticky tape, small freezer bag food labels.

What to do

Arrange closed cupboards and drawer units at right angles to the wall to create corners, areas and bays. Make these 'dividers' between the interest areas accessible to the children by removing as many doors as possible from cupboards etc and arranging the contents in labelled plastic storage baskets (available quite cheaply from hardware stores) or use ice-cream cartons.

A particularly attractive style of bookcase is the folding three-shelf variety, available from DIY furniture warehouses. They are light to carry and make airy dividers. The backs can be used for hanging booklets, storage pockets etc.

This kind of 'open plan' storage is possible also in 'movable' rooms. Use tea trolleys, book cases on casters and small open cupboards on wheels. As the baskets and cartons are quite deep, the contents will not fall out, even when the shelving is wheeled away for storage. Stick a strip of sugar paper in the designated interest area colour along the front of each open surface, and cover the strip with transparent film. Stick labels on to each basket or carton, again in the correct colour, with a picture and/or words. Make a matching label and stick it in the space beneath each basket or carton, so that if one is removed, the children know exactly where to return it, by matching the labels.

The theme area

What you need
A corner about 4 m x 2 m, a kitchen table or surplus teacher's desk, a sheet, home corner walls with door (not essential), home corner furniture, bookcase.

What to do
Arrange the home corner furniture in a corner of the room. Create a side 'wall' by using a kitchen table or surplus teacher's desk covered with a sheet. This can become a variety of imaginative hideaways for the children (mountain cave, squirrel's hole, tunnel, caravan etc). In self-service reception classes teachers often find they have less and less need for a teacher's desk, as the children become increasingly independent. The need to 'queue up' at the teacher's desk is eliminated, as the teacher moves about the classroom, observing the children's play,

Extend the length of the side 'wall' to at least 4 m, by using a bookcase etc. Omit the front 'wall' to the theme area, leaving it to open on to the creative floor play area. Children soon get used to this open plan arrangement. This will mean that the fantasy and role-play of the theme area can become an integral part of all the other activities in the room, and not a separate entity. Adults can feel inhibited about entering into children's imaginative play, especially if the adult has to squeeze through a child-sized door. The children, too, could find this intrusive; however, in an open-plan theme area there is no such physical barrier and both children and adults feel at ease, when the adult, after observing the children's play, participates as and when she feels appropriate, or when invited.

The creative floor play space

What you need

A space for wheeled toys and indoor 'activity' equipment (this provision is usually not found in reception classes); a space for building, with a carpet or blanket(s), or PE mats (if available); masking tape.

What to do

If you do not wish the children to ride around the whole room on their wheeled toys, define the limits of their 'territory' using masking tape. Similarly, in the building area, tell the children to keep within the area of the carpet, blanket(s) or mat(s). If the whole room is carpeted, then define the limits of this area by using masking tape, so avoiding long 'roads' and train tracks snaking their way across the room!

Storage

What you need
Deep open shelving or large storage box on wheels (M), wire supermarket type baskets (M), cardboard cartons or plastic storage boxes, drawer unit, bookcase for 'Miniature worlds' (see page 46), card, felt-tipped pens, sticky tape, covering film.

What to do
Sort out the bricks into different shapes and sizes and decide on appropriately shaped and sized cartons and boxes. Label each container with a card on which you have drawn an outline of the type of brick etc to be kept in the container and cover the label in transparent film. At 'tidy-up time', do not let the children simply put the bricks in each container in a jumbled heap, but ask them to lie them flat, side by side. This is a valuable exercise in spatial awareness.

For 'movable' rooms, it is usually not possible to provide enough portable storage. Instead, a large plastic box which is pulled along, or a wooden box on wheels in which all the bricks are piled together, is the best alternative. If this is the case, then encourage the children to place the bricks in flat, or one on top of the other, and not in a pile. For smaller bricks, baskets may be used. Stick a label on each basket showing the type of brick kept in the basket. Keep smaller construction toys in a numbered drawer unit.

The library

What you need
A two-seater settee if possible (on casters in 'movable' rooms) or a blanket chest or children's chairs covered with tie-on seat covers and backs, or folding garden chairs; cushions; floor-cushions; two bookcases; cardboard cartons covered in wallpaper; library display table; tablecloth or sheet; card; felt-tipped pens.

What to do
Beg or borrow a two-seater settee (ideal for shared/paired reading). If shabby, cover with old curtaining, a blanket or rug and some cushions. If a settee is not possible, improvise, using a blanket chest covered with cushions, against a wall.

Alternatively, cover children's chairs with tie-on covers, available cheaply from market stalls. Children's folding aluminium garden chairs are another alternative.

Divide the library from adjacent interest areas, such as the theme areas, by using a library display table, covered with a sheet of floor length table cloth. Store books not in use under this table, in wallpaper covered cartons. In reception classes, if your school colour codes books, use one box per colour level. Books could also be stored inside a lift-up blanket chest.

The listening corner

What you need

A quiet corner of the room, or a stockroom or corridor space, access to a power point, extension flex (if necessary), table, chairs, card, felt-tipped pens, storage for cassette tapes.

What to do

The listening corner is a quiet place where you and a child or two children may go to play listening games, tell a story to each other, or listen to stories, songs etc on a cassette recorder. Set up the items required. Include pictorial instructions on how to operate the recorder.

A pre-writing area (P) or a writing area (R)

What you need

A table near a wall for children to draw and write; blackboard paint; masking tape; a storage table covered with contact adhesive or a tablecloth or a set of shelves with ice-cream cartons, or a drawer unit; felt-tipped pens; freezer labels.

What to do

Paint an area with blackboard paint about a metre square from the ground up, on the wall by the writing table. Border it with masking tape. In a reception class reserve a space on the wall next to the blackboard area for wall pockets (see for example page 53).

Place necessary items on the storage table (see page 51 for details). Store items not in immediate use under the table.

Alternatively, use a set of shelves with labelled ice-cream cartons, or a drawer unit and wall chart, clearly labelled.

21

The maths area (R)

What you need
Three rectangular tables; storage in the form of open cupboards, shelving, drawer units etc; ice-cream cartons, baskets or trays.

What to do
Place two low open cupboards side by side at right angles to the wall, to form a divider. (If cupboards or shelving are unavailable, cover two rectangular tables with sheeting instead.) Store equipment not in current use out of sight underneath these tables in wallpaper covered cardboard boxes.

The top of these 'dividers' can be used as one of two 'maths interest' tables for pairs of children, or an adult and child, eg a weighing table and/or a table-top shop etc. In the main space, position the three rectangular tables together to form a large table for when you want to work with a group. When you have finished, the tables can easily be separated.

The art area

What you need
A tiled floor area (ideally); access to a sink; work table; easels; hooks for painting shirts etc; storage facilities eg doorless cupboards, sideboard, baby-changing unit, tea-trolley etc; contact adhesive covering; cardboard boxes; ice-cream cartons; card; felt-tipped pens.

What to do
Place the art table close to the storage facilities. Have everything clearly visible, labelled and accessible to the children so that they may help themselves to a wide

22

variety of 2-D and 3-D media, and creatively combine them. Let them be responsible for replenishing 'stock' by bringing in fresh junk items from home and refilling the containers when they see them getting 'low'. Large junk items such as cereal packets should be sorted and stacked neatly in separate, labelled cardboard boxes. Smaller items, for collage work etc can be kept in labelled ice-cream cartons. Remember to make two colour-coded labels one for every container and one for the space underneath the container.

Storage in 'permanent' rooms

Consider making an art 'pantry'. If you have an old-fashioned large heavy wooden storage cupboard, move it to the art area. Remove the doors and carefully arrange the contents in ice-cream cartons, plastic sweet jars etc so the children may help themselves from the lower area. Keep extra 'replenishing' stock eg tubs of powder paint, uncut paper etc on the higher shelves for adults' use. Alternatively, a bookcase, baby-changing unit or a tea trolley could be used.

Storage in 'movable' rooms

The problem of providing efficient storage of this 'open plan' kind is, of course, greater in 'movable' rooms; however, many imaginative solutions can be found. If funds do not stretch to a purpose-built metal art trolley on wheels then one or more bookcases on casters, filled with labelled ice-cream cartons will be suitable. Other ideas include a large old-fashioned wooden dinner wagon, a baby-changing unit fitted with casters, vegetable racks and tea trolleys, all filled with ice-cream cartons.

23

The quiet area

What you need

Two rectangular tables, open shelving with ice-cream cartons and/or number and colour-coded drawer unit for storage of 'table-toys' etc; old free-standing photograph frames; card; magazine or educational suppliers catalogue pictures; felt-tipped pens.

What to do

The quiet area is for activities which may be carried out only on the table eg jigsaws, play figures and objects which could be broken if trodden on the floor, bead threading, mosaics, sewing and pre-maths equipment with other maths resources in the maths area (see page 22).

Place the two tables together to form a group for four children. You can separate the tables so that pairs of children or an adult and a child have the opportunity to work together.

Have pictures showing children working with the construction toys, mosaics etc similar to those provided. In addition to the main poster 'advertising' the quiet area, make mini-display notices, each showing a different game etc being used. Place these in old photograph frames and change from day to day to spark off ideas. For further ideas on adult involvement with children's play in the quiet area see page 65.

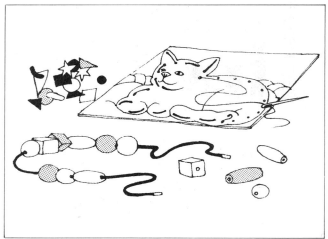

The discovery area

What you need
Two sand trays, a water trough, two vegetable racks, table or open cupboard, adhesive contact covering, storage baskets and labels, facilities for growing plants etc and keeping small animals on a temporary or permanent basis.

What to do
Arrange wet and dry sand trays and a water trough next to vegetable racks containing sand and water play equipment. Ideally, these should be on a tiled floor, near to a sink, possibly near to the art area. Cover a table or open cupboard top with contact covering, ideally in your discovery area colour. Under the table or on the cupboard shelves arrange labelled 'discovery baskets', each containing a collection of related items for the children to investigate:

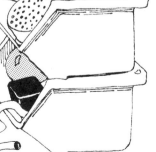

The cloakroom

What you need

Card, felt-tipped pens, clear transparent film, sugar paper, photocopier, children's photographs.

What to do
Pre-school children

Write each child's name on a card, with a picture. Cover with transparent film and stick next to each peg. Write all the children's names on a large sheet of card, together with their pictures, and stick on the cloakroom wall. In addition, make a set of name cards, which can be held up one at a time for the children to recognise. Also make a set of the pictures used, again for holding up. Use the name cards and picture cards, in conjunction with the wall chart, for a variety of games. For example hold up a name card and say 'This person please go and put on your coat' etc.

Reception children

If possible allow two pegs per child, one for a coat, and one for a school bag and/or PE bag. Make a card for each peg, with the child's name and a number. Group children's names according to the initial letter of their first name, starting with 'A' eg Alison, Anwar etc. Point this out to the children and use as a basis for games; 'All the children whose names begin with 'G' go and get your coats please'. These games are a useful way of organising the children in the cloakroom. The numbers of children using the cloakroom at any one time can be regulated using these games so that a crowded mêlée is avoided (see also Chapter 2). In addition, make a wall chart of the children's names and cloakroom numbers, and make a set of name cards and number cards, for cloakroom games.

Out-of-doors

What you need

Direct access to an enclosed play area; a covered sand pit or covered sand-filled tyre; grassy area (if possible); small garden area (if possible); permanently fixed 'adventure' equipment eg tree trunk 'stepping stones', climbing log or frame etc.

What to do

Opportunities for running, jumping, climbing, pushing and pulling etc are necessary for the development of physical, social, imaginative and problem-solving skills. Playgroups and nurseries provide indoor 'activity' equipment, in the form of indoor slides, see-saws, 'sit 'n' ride' vehicles etc and an enclosed outdoor play area is always provided. Four-year-olds in the reception class also need the opportunity for this kind of challenging, structured, physical play and every effort should be made to ensure that adequate staffing and resources are provided.

Permanently fixed, large outdoor play equipment along with the necessary supervisory personnel should be a feature of reception classes as well as pre-schools. In some reception classes where there is a nursery class on the same site, it may be possible for the reception children to have access to this equipment, through nursery, reception teachers and other qualified staff working together to arrange a rota of shared supervision. In addition to large items of equipment, many smaller, often improvised items, can be used to create a stimulating outdoor environment.

The self-service room

Chapter two

Resourcing the self-

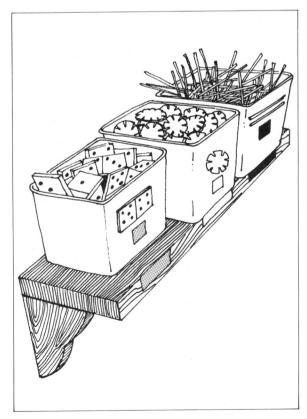

The self-service room is designed to maximise the opportunities for children to become independent, creative learners. The principle of having resources clearly visible and easily accessible is as important for the adults as it is for the children. Having the distinctive interest areas and their related resources helps children in their decision-making. In the workshop atmosphere of the self-service classroom, you are able to observe the children's differing developmental learning needs, and can recognise any critical learning 'moment' and exploit it fully, by having instant access to a wide range of resources.

The self-service room encourages creativity by enabling children to combine different materials and resources. It is therefore very important that everything should be easily returnable to its original place through the use of colour coding. Have extra card for colour coding at hand, so that new items can be instantly coded. Having all resources visible and accessible does not mean that children should have access to everything all the time. This can cause confusion and indecision, as children become 'spoilt for choice', and can lead to superficial concentration. Keep all items not in current use in a separate place which is still visible and accessible, so that you do not forget about them.

In addition to commercially produced resources the self-service room makes good use of many home-made and 'real' items.

Visit jumble sales, charity shops and car boot sales. Keep parents in regular touch with topics, via letters, and ask for any relevant items which parents may be able to spare either permanently or on loan.

service room

Structured play in the self-service room

'The education of young children is founded in play'. (*Better Schools* March 1985, paragraph 123, HMSO). The self-service room is planned to provide an enriching play environment, in which the children have much opportunity to decide for themselves what to do and to work independently. The purpose of enabling children to play without the direct supervision of adults is not to ensure that adults can 'work' uninterrupted with small groups. The value of play as an educational experience is dependent upon the structuring role of adults in providing and arranging resources and in carefully observing the children as they play, interacting with them through language in order to support and extend the learning potential inherent in the play.

'The teacher helps the children consolidate their abilities in developmentally appropriate ways, through direct and representational experience, without trying to accelerate their development or push them along to the next level. The teacher asks questions of the children about their plans, intentions, experiences and observations. When the teacher 'tests' the children, the purpose is to gather information, so that the children will have maximum support for independent learning. Each child is recognised as an individual who builds his or her own knowledge through initiatives shared with supportive adults. Which is to say, each child is *active* .' (Foreword, *Young Children in Action* by Mary Hohmann, Bernard Banet and David P Weikart, The High/Scope Press).

Talking with children

The value of enabling children to plan their activities in advance, as they look at the opportunities available in all the interest areas, and to talk about them afterwards, is now widely recognised. Suggestions for helping children develop these skills through conversation may be found in 'The getting together area' (see page 15). In addition, you can observe and talk with individual children about their self-chosen activities in each interest area. It is helpful for you to have in the back of your mind a simple framework of 'pointers' for talking with children about their play. A very succinct description of these 'pointers' appears in the curriculum checklists of *Young Children in Action*. You will find these checklists very useful in helping to observe children's play closely. Using this knowledge, you will be able to help children plan for an activity and see it through, solving problems along the way, and also to represent and communicate experiences to others. The development of all these cognitive skills will provide a firm foundation for the kind of learning emphasised in the National Curriculum.

The getting together area

Let's get together

What you need
A space large enough for all the children to sit together, often in a circle.

What to do
The getting together area is a space where individuals, pairs, small groups or all the children together may enjoy floor activities other than those in the creative floor play space. Some children prefer working on the floor to the table, for example, when playing snap with a partner. Ideally, if space permits, the getting together area should be in addition to the creative floor play space. This is so that you can take aside a small group of children and sit with them on the floor and play, say, a language game, sing songs, or watch the children as they handle certain kinds of building blocks, or floor jigsaws, without disturbing the work of others in the creative floor play space. The getting together area can do double duty as the creative floor play space, but constructions may have to be dismantled in order to allow everyone to sit down. In this case, always give a 'five minute warning', before tidying up time, and advise the builders not to start any new projects.

The getting together area is also suitable for gathering children together to help them plan their activities and remember and describe them later. Once the children are familiar with the layout of the room and the resources, you can ask each child what he would like to do, and how he is going to do it. You will have to give an appropriate amount of guidance to each child so that she is gradually

encouraged to discuss her plans in an increasing amount of detail.

In pre-school situations the children can sit in small groups with one adult per group who will help each child to plan his activities and help him to get started. The adult may then keep track of children in his group as they play, observing and discussing the children's activities with them, and then, later, gather the same group together and help the children to recall and describe their activities to each other. In reception classes, the children may sit in a circle while each child is asked her plans. Similarly, later on the children may sit in a circle while each child is asked to recall his activities. The reception teacher need not worry if every child does not get the opportunity to recall his experiences every day, so long as he remembers to see that the child has a turn the next day.

The getting together area may be used also for stories, singing, music making and games with the whole group together at one time. When the children are all together, it is often a good idea to sit them in a circle. This encourages socialisation as all the children can see one another and be encouraged to listen to each other and take turns. Many singing, language, action and miming games can be played in which each child has a turn.

A circle ensures that nobody is left out and the less confident children can initially copy others in 'having a go', gradually developing confidence.

Display table

What you need
Table or set of shelves or 3-tier tea trolley; card; felt-tipped pens; two shallow boxes or tidy drawers (R); pencils; paper; card; crayons in a box (R).

What to do
Young children love to bring favourite toys, objects, books etc to pre-school or school. As well as providing a valuable insight into a child's interests, these objects can be used also to help children plan their activities. A child may bring a teddy for example, and wish to dress it up to take it to a party in the theme area. These objects from home, together with models etc which a child makes may be displayed on the display table, and shown to others at recall time. You can write the child's name or a simple caption and place it by the model.

Young children delight in adult approval and need to 'show' an adult what they have produced straightaway. This can present a problem for the reception teacher who is usually busy. When free, discuss the models etc with the individual children, or wait until the end of the session for recall time. Prepare a sign showing the children where to place their models etc. Have a small box on the display table containing paper, small cards, pencils and crayons, for those children who are able to write their own names, labels or speech bubbles to put next to their models. Also on the display table, or underneath, put out two tidy drawers, one labelled 'Finished Work', and one 'Unfinished Work'. If children produce work on paper (pictures) or in a book, and you are not available to see it immediately, they can place their work in the 'Finished Work' box for you to see as soon as you are free.

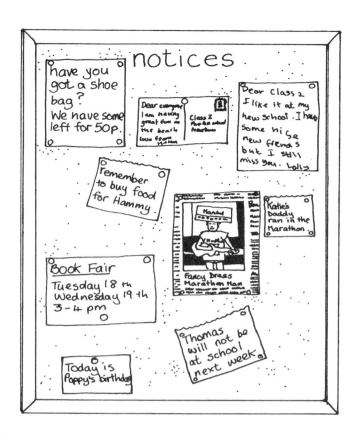

What's news today?

What you need
A notice-board, drawing pins.

What to do
Each morning, pin up an interesting and/or amusing notice or letter. You can also use it to pin up examples from the real world which you can discuss with the children eg letters from parents, postcards, local newspaper cuttings etc. Encourage the children to bring notice-board items in from home, too. Use it as a genuine reminder to yourself, and let the children see you writing messages to yourself eg 'Don't forget to buy fish food' (for the classroom goldfish). Use it also to announce forthcoming events.

The surprise box

What you need
A large cardboard box, white paper, pictures of toys and TV characters cut from magazines, transparent covering film, ribbon.

What to do
Make an attractive surprise box by covering a large box with white paper. Cut out pictures of toys and television and cartoon characters and stick them on to the white paper. Cover with transparent film for durability. Affix a colourful ribbon around the box, gift style, and stick an enormous bow on one of the top flaps, so the box looks like a permanently wrapped present.

The magic blanket

What you need
Enough large blankets for the whole group to sit together.

What to do
If you are unable to have a carpet in the getting together area, use blankets instead. Using blankets means also that the getting together area can be flexibly positioned if you require. If you wish to highlight a particular interest area, as part of a theme, you can temporarily enlarge that area by moving back the 'dividers' (cupboards, drawer units etc) and placing the blankets on the floor inside the interest area. Even if your getting together area is carpeted, using blankets occasionally can add a touch of adventure. Climbing aboard the 'magic' blankets to listen to a story, helps set an exciting anticipatory mood and can inspire children's imaginations - 'Let's pretend this is a flying carpet!'.

Since blankets can be slippery on polished floors, it is best not to allow small groups of children to use them unsupervised. Use them only when an adult can ensure that the children come to sit on them gently and safely, and not in a scramble.

The theme area
Enlarging the home corner

What to do

The home corner could be developed into a theme area, in order to give the children an opportunity for a wide variety of fantasy and role-play. A theme area also makes it much easier for an adult to become involved in children's imaginative play in a non-dominant role. The theme area differs from the traditional home corner in several respects. Firstly, it is larger, since a space in front of the home furniture is left free to become another multi-purpose imaginary setting. Secondly, unlike the traditional home corner, the theme area should not be shut off from the rest of the room and the vision of adult(s). As the theme area is open to the rest of the room, it is much easier for adult(s) to take an interest in the children's dramatic play, to talk with them and develop their ideas and vocabulary just as they do in other areas of learning. Without an adult's interest, children's play can stagnate and valuable opportunities for informal learning and language development will be missed. The theme area makes it possible for a theme to extend into children's fantasy and role play, their natural medium of learning. The ideas which follow serve as an introduction to the role of the adult, and also describe what is needed to equip a theme area. Elaborate costumes are not essential. Everything necessary can be improvised quickly and easily even by one reception teacher working without help. The theme area may be called the 'dressing-up' area or whatever it happens to be at the time eg fire station, hospital, aeroplane etc.

Home corner furniture

What you need

Commercially produced home corner furniture with cupboard doors removed; an ordinary children's table, slightly smaller than usual (if possible a round one is ideal); classroom chairs; as much open shelving as possible to house items; plastic baskets; labels; cardboard boxes; gloss paint; Stanley knife; sticky tape; felt-tipped pens.

What to do

There should always be a home corner section of the theme area. If possible, try to make all the storage in the theme area open plan, colour coded and labelled, like the rest of the room.

Accessibility to costumes, props etc can greatly enhance the quality of children's play. Arrange the furniture at one end of the theme area, possibly along two walls, with the round table in the corner. Position one or two classroom chairs (with padded covers if possible) at the table. The table may be left in the corner, or occasionally brought out into the middle of the home corner area. (Because of the extra space provided in the multi-purpose play space, the children still have plenty of room to play, even with the table in the centre.) Extra domestic appliances, such as a television, video, fridge, microwave oven and washing machine can all be made quite easily from cardboard boxes, painted with gloss paint. Do not have all the appliances in use at once. As with all items in the theme area, 'ring the changes' to maintain the children's interest and curiosity and even home made items will last surprisingly well. Make a cardboard bookshelf for easy to read books in the home corner space.

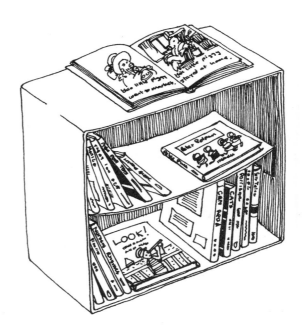

Props

What you need

Two telephones (real if possible), telephone directory, pencils, messages pad, calendar, magazine pictures, card, felt-tipped pens, magazines (especially TV) and comics, magazine rack, adult size unbreakable tea set (eg picnic set), real stainless steel teapot, real stainless steel coffee jug, real cutlery (see that knives are blunt), unbreakable condiment set, pans (graded in size), kitchen utensils (whisk, spatula, ladle etc), baking equipment, pretend food, items for 'shops', dolls, cuddly toys for 'pets', cardboard boxes for extra cots, bedding, puppets, cleaning equipment (dusters, tea towels etc), 'baby' items (empty 'talc' bottle, Velcro 'nappies' etc).

What to do

Provide real items for children to play at reading and writing activities taken from real life eg 'copying' a recipe, making shopping lists, being a doctor's receptionist and taking down telephone messages etc. Once children can form letters correctly in the reception class, add picture cards of shopping items in the home corner space for them to copy. Keep these in a file index box, like 'cookery cards'. Sometimes arrange the table as a writing table with plenty of space to write. At other times, let the children put the writing materials away on a shelf and use the table for other purposes eg a meal etc.

Try to arrange the storage of props as carefully as all other resources. For example, you could have plastic baskets on open shelves. Each basket could be labelled eg 'baby clothes'. Make a set of duplicate labels and stick them on the shelves, so that children know where to return each basket.

Cooking in the theme area

What you need

Real ingredients, appropriate utensils, 'play' food (eg empty packets stuffed with newspaper, having stickdown flaps for stability), tins, cartons, foam or wooden 'chips' (stress dangers of putting in mouth), milk bottle-tops, conkers, plastic fruit and vegetables, magazine pictures of food, card, felt-tipped pens, ice-cream carton.

What to do

Cooking in the theme area can be of two kinds – food preparation with real ingredients in the presence of an adult (eg making sandwiches, fruit salads, preparing cakes and biscuits etc) and children's pretend cooking. The first can inspire the second. Prepare colourful 'menu cards' with a picture of a meal on a plate with simple words underneath. Keep these in an ice-cream carton, rather like a cook's index file, to inspire children when they're thinking about 'what to make for tea'.

Banana Crunchies

You need—
3 bananas, crunchy cereal, golden syrup, water, cocktail sticks.
To make—
Add 2 spoons of syrup to 2 spoons of water and warm over a low heat.
Peel the bananas and cut in half.
Stick a cocktail stick into each and dip the bananas into the syrup mixture.
Then dip the bananas into the cereal a...

Egg and Cress Sandwiches

You need —
Eggs, sliced bread, butter, cress
To make —
Hard boil the eggs for 6 minutes.
Crack and take off the egg shell.
Chop and mix the egg in a bowl.
Spread butter and egg onto the sliced bread and add some cress.

Multi-purpose space

What you need
Cardboard cartons, Stanley knife, card, felt-tipped pens, one or more small 'sit n'ride' vehicles, various everyday props related to theme (eg soft toys), bricks from building area, classroom chairs, string or skipping rope.

What to do
A multi-purpose play space, in addition to the home-base, can easily be created by sticking a few notices and signs on a wall nearby eg 'surgery', 'fire station' etc and by adding a few extra chairs and large upturned cartons, suitably marked with a felt-tipped pen (eg a doctor's receptionist's 'desk'). This space can enrich the children's dramatic play by providing other imaginary settings. For example, the children could prepare the 'food' for a picnic in the home base and then go into the 'forest' (multi-purpose play space) equipped with table cloth etc.

Sometimes you could combine the theme area and the building area, for example by creating a hospital, using bricks and cartons from the building area as beds for the dolls. Bricks and cartons can be used also for walls, castles, boats etc.

Dressing-up clothes

What you need
Old clothes, hats and bags, sheets, lengths of material, Velcro, needle, cotton, child-sized trouser hangers, washing line, string, sugar paper, card, foil, sticky tape, felt-tipped pens, gold or silver buttons.

What to do
Young children can find the task of rummaging through a dressing-up box a little daunting, and can eventually come to ignore the box altogether. It is preferable to have a smaller number of clothes, changed regularly, which are visible and easily accessible to the children. Many children find even child-sized hangers difficult to cope with. An alternative idea is to use child-sized trouser hangers, and teach the children simply to slot the garment through the space. Use one garment per hanger, and tie each hanger securely to the back of a piece of furniture (eg bookcase), or fix a washing line on to a wall, and tie the hangers on to that.

Costumes, perhaps related to a theme can easily be improvised. Use lengths of material with Velcro, for long wrap-over skirts, capes, trains etc. Replace all tie-on tapes (eg on aprons) with Velcro. Existing hats can become uniform hats by sticking on cardboard or foil badges with sticky tape. To create a flat topped hat for a postman, bus driver etc simply take a child's baseball type hat and sew on top a circle of double thickness blue sugar paper. Sew a band of blue paper round the side, and add a milk bottle top for the front badge. A multi-purpose uniform jacket can be created from a child's blazer or raincoat. Sew on gold or silver buttons. For animals, make a rectangular headband out of sugar paper, and add appropriately coloured and sized ears.

Many children are happy simply to have a cardboard badge stuck on to their clothes with sticky tape to denote who they are.

Give careful thought to how the provision of clothes can reinforce gender stereotyping. For example try to provide 'unisex' nurses' uniforms (a shirt with collar removed, worn back to front with a Velcro fastening; a motif such as a red cross can be sewn on a pocket at the front). Encourage both boys and girls to be nurses and doctors. Provide many different styles of clothing, such as saris and kaftans.

witches
and
wizards

doctors
nurses

farms

Theme bags

What you need
Plastic carrier bags, sticky labels, felt-tipped pens.

What to do
As you build up your supplies of simple costumes and props, it is useful to keep certain key items in labelled bags, away from the children, in an accessible place. A witches' and wizards' bag, for example, could contain black cloaks, plastic spiders and frogs and a spell book. Over a period of time, it becomes quite easy to locate the items you want at short notice.

Adults can feel inhibited about involving themselves in children's fantasy and role-play because they do not wish to stifle their imaginations. There are, however, many ways in which adults can be appropriately involved in this play, through conversation, which will enhance the quality of the play without dominating it. For example, when asked what she would like to do, a child may say she wants to be a doctor. You can then encourage her to talk about the kinds of things a doctor does.

It is important that an adult can observe the children's play in the theme area, and so be able to decide on an appropriate moment to be involved. The absence of a front wall in the theme area makes this observation possible.

If there is a full-scale topic in which everyone is involved for that day (eg if the theme area has become a cafe or doctor's surgery etc), then the adults can plan with the whole group at the beginning of the morning, who they (the adults) could be. Additionally, an adult may sit with a small group and give each person a puppet or 'playmobile' figure to stimulate ideas and vocabulary for role-play later on.

Creative floor play space

A building store

What you need

Planks (large and small), wooden and plastic bricks, cardboard cartons, train set, carpet square samples, junk items, chalk, skipping rope, masking tape, lengths of sheet, blue and green plain fabric, Action Man and Sindy or Barbie dolls, Tonka toys (brought from home for the day).

What to do

Encourage the children to combine commercially produced building items with junk items and small floor toys. Let the children use carpet square samples as bases for separate buildings, double skipping ropes for roads, sheets over inclined planks as ski runs and blue and green fabric for seas and grass.

Occasionally take some 'dolls' and a small group of children. Sit with them on the floor and encourage ideas for 'adventures' which can then be played out in the building areas. They can use the bricks for making houses, garages, vehicles, roads, buildings, mountains, forests, lakes etc connected with their dolls' adventures.

Many valuable opportunities for discussing concepts of spatial awareness can arise from conversations with children about their work in the building area. For example, give each child in a group one carpet square as a 'foundation' for a house. Ask each child to use bricks to build the walls (leaving a space for the door) and observe how each child tackles the problem of fitting the bricks side by side to match the size of the square.

Floor toy cabinet

What you need

A drawer unit, cars, felt-tipped pens, small toys (selections of which are durable enough to be played with on the floor), small sticky labels.

What to do

There are many small construction toys and games which are durable enough to be played with either on the table, or on the floor. Give the children the opportunity to do both. Keep these toys together in a numbered and labelled drawer unit at the side of the carpeted building area, and away from fragile toys which may be played with only on the table. Using durable small toys in this way greatly enhances their play potential, as children have much greater opportunity and space to use their imaginations. If children are to be encouraged to mix different sets of toys, it is very important that the toys can be put back quickly in their correct places.

Suggestions for the kinds of durable floor toys to keep in the drawer unit are Lego, Sticklebricks, Mobilo, Multilink, Unifix cubes, Constructo straws, jungle animals, farm animals, toy cars, space people, dinosaurs, certain strong kinds of play people, small wooden villages etc.

Miniature worlds

What you need
A bookcase or cardboard cartons, white sugar paper, magazine pictures, adhesive, staples, felt-tipped pens, sets of small toys eg jungle or farm animals, toy cars, space people, dinosaurs, play people etc; home-made models eg made from Plasticine, junk items etc.

What to do
Use each shelf of a bookcase to house a different set of small toys. Draw an appropriate background for each 'miniature world' either yourself, or with the children. Use felt-tipped pens and magazine pictures. For example, one shelf could be a jungle scene, one shelf a farm scene, and one shelf a space 'world'. Allow one or two children to play at a time.

The library
Reading is fun

What you need
A plentiful supply of attractive books including 'Big Books' (see page 96), an easel, two bulldog clips.

What to do
When children first start playgroup, nursery or school, it is important to attract them into the library corner, and to take practical steps to encourage them to stay there, even if an adult is not present. Try to arrange, wherever possible, for another reader to sit in the library, such as a

classroom assistant, parent, grandparent or teenager. Explain to helpers the importance of talking about the pictures, asking, 'What do you think might happen next?' and encouraging some children to retell parts of the story. Encourage the children to share books. In reception classes, if a child chooses a particular book and you know another child can read it, ask the second child to read it to the first, or to read it out loud together. If 'Big books' are available, sit with a small group of children in the library and share it with them. Attach the 'Big book' to an easel with bulldog clips (a painting easel is ideal, since the clip-on paint tray at the bottom gives additional support to the weight of the book). After you have read with a small group, individual children may enjoy playing 'teacher' and reading to others.

It is well worth encouraging the children to take pleasure in looking at pictures and talking about them. Even if children cannot read a book, those who have been encouraged to do so, will still enjoy poring over the pictures and 'telling the story to themselves'. Have a good supply of books without words in order to introduce this skill. Let the children take those home, with a short letter explaining to parents how they might talk about them with their children.

In a reception class it is a good idea to put on the shelves only those books which the children have read before and/or very simple books which you know they will be able to read on their own, especially rhythmic and repetitive books. Children love to re-read those 'old favourites' many times over. This builds up confidence and a love of the reading habit. Change the books every day. Display them with their front covers facing outwards. Display enough books for one book per child with a few extra. Store other books not currently in use.

Choosing and returning books

What you need
Two boxes or drawer trays or baskets, card, felt-tipped pens.

What to do
Label one box 'Returned books' and one box 'Books to go home'. Place the first box by the door each morning. As the children come in, they can place their book in the box. Put the second box in the library. When a child chooses a book and has read it, he can put it in the 'Books to go home' box. No other child may then choose this book, and disputes are avoided. As often as you can, pop into the library and check through the books in the box and either read or discuss them with the children.

Book slips (R)

What you need
Duplicated sheets, scissors, paper clips.

What to do
It can be helpful to send home a 'book slip' with certain books. This slip, attached to the front of the book with a paper clip, indicates how parents might best use a particular book with their child, on that evening. Examples of four different kinds of slips are shown here.

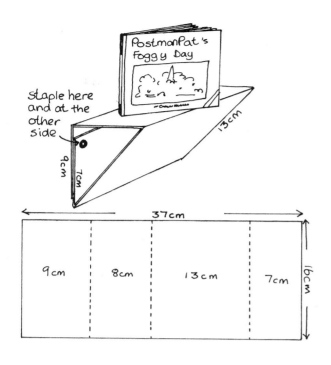

Wall book display shelf

What you need
Piece of card 37cm × 16cm; white and coloured paper; felt-tipped pens; children's drawings, paintings, writing, models and mobiles connected to book themes.

What to do
Make the library as visually attractive as possible. Books can be displayed on the wall by the use of a card shelf. Fold the card to form a 3-D shelf to hold a book (see illustration). Add mounted displays of children's work, both 2-D and 3-D, related to book themes.

A book table

What you need
A table, piece of floor-length material, books, related objects eg soft toys, card, felt-tipped pens.

What to do
Cover a table with floor length material and display sets of books on a particular topic eg 'Spot' books, together with any related items the children may bring from home or make at school eg a 'Spot' soft toy, a dog dish with dog biscuits, a rubber bone etc. Add labels written by you, or the children. Sometimes, the theme on the book table can be developed in the theme area eg children can devise a scenario about Spot getting lost. Children could use these props in the theme area. Information books about people's jobs also make interesting displays and can inspire children's role-play in the theme area.

The listening corner

Record and listen

What you need
Cassette recorder; headphones or earphones; home-made or commercial tapes of short, well-loved stories, songs and rhymes; home-made or published books to match the tapes; coloured sticky labels (eg those used for colour-coding); card; felt-tipped pens; musical instruments (eg percussion) both commercial and home-made.

What to do
Stick labels on three of the buttons on the cassette recorder eg red for stop, green for play, blue for rewind etc. Make a large poster to explain the procedure and teach pairs of children how to operate the recorder.

Although musical instruments can be kept in the discovery area you can keep them in the listening corner too. Encourage individuals and pairs of children to make up a short, simple rhythm with the instruments and record it. Then see if others can listen to it, and copy it.

A pre-writing area (P) or a writing area (R)

The stationery store

What you need

A table for drawing and writing; chairs, shelving or a storage table on which to keep items in constant use; ice-cream cartons or small bread baskets; labels; pencils (thick and thin); wax crayons (thick and thin); felt-tipped pens; rulers; erasers; attractive metal trays or shallow tidy boxes; paper in different colours, shapes and sizes; ready-made booklets in various colours, shapes and sizes; chalks; boards; tracing paper; picture and paper clips; jumbo typewriter.

What to do

Arrange the items, labelled on shelving etc. Explain to the children that they can help themselves to what they need from the 'stationery store'. Train them to return the items correctly, otherwise the drawing/writing table can become cluttered. If possible, use small bread baskets for pencils, crayons etc.

Use this area for encouraging children to record either in picture form, and/or in words, what they do. For example, if a child has built a brick train, he appreciates that he cannot take it home but might enjoy drawing a picture of it.

Do not, of course, insist that he draws a picture and/or writes about it every time. Let an adult sit in this corner and be a 'secretary' who will write down whatever children may wish to dictate (stories, a letter home about what they had for dinner today etc) and read it back to them.

More stationery

What you need

'Magic slates' (available from newsagents and toy shops), a photograph album with plastic overlay sheets or slip-in transparent pockets, white sugar paper, felt-tipped pen, a cloth, small salt tray, small sand tray, any commercially produced materials, plain paper bulletin books (if used).

What to do

Store the above items, ideally in a numbered drawer unit. Make a letter formation album, by drawing each letter on white sugar paper, showing the starting point. Slip the letters in the album in alphabetical order. In the reception class, if a child is having problems forming a particular letter, the letter can be instantly located in the album, and the child can write on the top of the plastic overlay sheet with a water soluble felt-tipped pen, which can be wiped off. This idea can be used to teach number formation, too. Commercially produced 'magic slates' can be used in the same way as the photograph album. Children can also practise letter formation by tracing letters with their fingers in a small tray of salt or sand. If bulletin books are used they can be kept in some of the drawers for the children to locate as necessary.

Alphabet pockets

What you need

Two sets of hanging plastic shoe pockets (12 pockets per set and available from hardware stores), large white sticky labels, felt-tipped pens, a wide variety of alphabet letters eg wooden, plastic, sandpaper, magnetic, 'feely' etc.

What to do

Fit the two sets of hanging plastic shoe pockets side by side on the wall, possibly next to the blackboard space. On the front of each pocket, stick a label, on which you have written an alphabet letter, together with a picture of an object beginning with that letter. The last two pockets will have to 'double-up' with letters. Write the letters in alphabetical order. Give a group of children a letter each and see if they can return it to its correct pocket.

The magnetic board

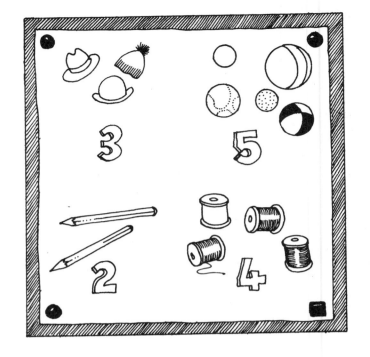

What you need

A large magnetic board, sheets of thin white paper, sticky tape, mastic adhesive or a bulldog clip, felt-tipped pens.

What to do

Fix a board to the wall, ideally next to the alphabet pockets if space permits. If not, fix the board to the back of a 'divider', such as a bookcase. Each day, fix a large piece of paper on top of the board, and with felt-tipped pens, draw simple pictures. Children can work out the initial letters of the pictures, find them in the alphabet pockets, and place them under the correct pictures. Adapt this idea to your children's interests and needs, and let them draw pictures for you and other children to find the initial letter. Use this idea with magnetic numbers too. Draw sets of objects and children have to place the correct magnetic numbers under each set.

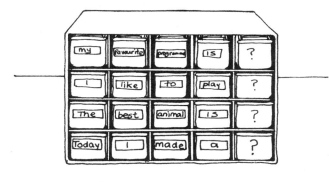

The word box (R)

What you need
A tool storage cabinet with transparent plastic drawers (sold at DIY stores for storing nails, screws etc), or five transparent plastic cassette cases and card, felt-tipped pens.

What to do
The word box serves as an easy-to-use device for introducing children to simple composing skills. Stick a word on the front of each drawer with copies of the same word inside. For example, 'my favourite programme is...'. Stick a question mark on the front of the fifth drawer. Inside keep blank slips of card or paper for you to write the child's favourite programme, food etc. Place the word box on the writing table and let children select and replace the cards they need for writing. When not in use, keep the word box on the storage shelves. If a tool cabinet is unavailable a home-made word-holder can easily be made by opening a cassette box to its fullest, so that it stands up like a mini book stand. Stick about five of these together in a row with sticky tape, use as a sentence holder by placing different word cards in each box.

Word pockets (R)

What you need
Two or more sets of shoe pockets, card, felt-tipped pens, paper clips, large sticky labels.

What to do
Word pockets will help to avoid long queues of children waiting for you to write a word for them for their stories etc. Fix the pockets to the wall in the writing corner, if space permits, or to the back of a 'divider'. Once the children are proficient in the use of the word box, they can be introduced to the word pockets. Stick an alphabet label on each pocket (see on page 53, 'Alphabet pockets'), and inside each pocket keep a selection of different words all beginning with the pocket letter (one word per card). If necessary, illustrate the cards. Devise games to teach the children how to locate the pocket they need. Get the children to select the word(s) they need for their writing and replace in the correct pocket. Write a question mark on the front of the last pocket and keep blank cards in it, for you to write extra words. If there is room, a third set of pockets can be used to house 'families' of words, eg 'colour' words, 'toys', family names, days of the week etc.

The maths area (R)

Although a separate maths area is appropriate only in reception classes, some of the following ideas may be of interest to pre-school teachers and leaders.

The maths store

What you need

A table-top cooker (out of children's reach), open and colour-coded storage for cookery equipment and ingredients, measuring resources, balance scales and weighing objects, 2-D and 3-D shapes and 'real' items, items for shops, money (plastic and real), real and commercially produced items for pre-number and number relations concepts, home-made or commercially produced flip-chart, plain paper books, duplicated work sheets, published maths work book.

What to do

Arrange for the flexible use of the resources by individuals and pairs at the 'maths interest' tables and also by small groups of children and a teacher at the group maths table in the centre of the area. This table can be used for activities such as cooking (although this can be carried out also in the theme area occasionally, and the recording of maths work).

Maths interest tables

What you need

Two or more classroom tables, various practical equipment (see page 57).

What to do

In addition to the group maths table in the centre of the maths area, arrange around the sides several 'maths interest' tables. These can provide activities for individuals and pairs of children. Activities can be introduced to a group, and then followed up individually or in pairs at the interest tables. The interest tables provide children with the opportunity to explore different mathematical areas in their own way and at their own pace, either on their own or with a partner. You will have a chance to observe their behaviour and talk at length with the children. Vary the kinds of maths interest tables and also the nature of the activities on each table according to your children's needs and interests. Ideas for interest tables include a counting or matching table, a pairs game table, a weighing table, a measuring table and a shape table.

Name tubs

What you need
A cottage cheese pot per child, sticky labels, felt-tipped pen, card, collection of objects to sort.

What to do
Using sticky labels, write each child's name on a cottage cheese pot. Call these pots 'name tubs'. Introduce the activity by folding over a piece of card so it stands up, and writing a pictorial instruction on it, such as 'make a set of red things'. Watch the children as they select items you have put out on the table, or let them find articles from anywhere in the room. Each child puts her set in her name tub. Discuss each child's set with her. Gather small groups of children together frequently to discuss each other's set. See if other children can work out how a child has made his set. If not, ask the child to explain it.

Number pockets

What you need
One set of plastic hanging shoe pockets, sticky labels, felt-tipped pen, different kinds of numerals eg wooden, plastic, sandpaper, magnetic, 'jelly' etc.

What to do
Fix pockets to a wall and add labels on the front. Number the labels 0 to 10. Place all the numerals in the appropriate pockets. Encourage the children to go to these pockets for the numerals they need for whatever purpose eg drawing round, copying, adding to displays, for use with the magnetic board etc.

A table-top shop

What you need

A large egg carton, shopping bag, purse, sorting tray, real coins, scissors, wrapping paper, transparent covering film, card, felt-tipped pens, carrier bags from well known stores, relevant real objects, string, hole punch.

What to do

Cut the carton into the shape of an usherette's tray with sloping sides, keeping the original size of the bottom of the carton. Cover with colourful wrapping paper and transparent film for extra strength. Collect bags from well-known toy shops, chemists, clothes shops, book shops, baby chainstores etc. In each bag put a selection of items that can be bought from each store eg toys, chemist's requisites etc. Tie a price tag (in pennies) to each item. Make a card for each shop, sticking on the name of the shop cut from a spare carrier bag. Affix the card to the back of the table top shop with paper clips. Keep the bags visible so that the children can choose what sort of shop they would like. Other ideas for shops include a card shop (children must sort cards into sets by age, or type eg 'get well' etc) and a real fruit and vegetable shop. Change the stock in the shop quite often. It can frequently be related to a classroom theme eg for a pet/vet theme, have a pet shop using small soft toy animals.

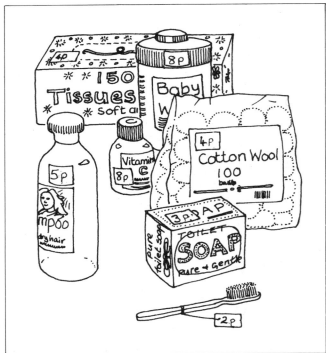

60

The art area

Crafty smocks

What you need
Old shirts, scissors, Velcro, tape, needle and cotton.

What to do
Use an old shirt with sleeves cut down. Sew approximately 5 cm Velcro (preferably in a bright colour) about 15 cm down from the neck to fasten the shirt instead of buttons. Sew a piece of tape to form a hanging loop inside the collar. Teach the children how to hang up the shirts by the loop. You will find that they become completely independent in helping one another to put them on.

Disposable non-spill paint pots

What you need
Ice-cream cartons, yoghurt pots, scissors, paper, sticky tape.

What to do
A very time-consuming task is washing out paint pots. If your children are regularly bringing in supplies of yoghurt pots to replenish the art pantry, then consider using these as disposable paint pots. Place four in an ice-cream carton. Fill each pot with paint. Cut holes in the carton lid slightly smaller than the circumference of each pot so they protrude slightly.

Fix-it drawers

What you need

One tool storage box with transparent
drawers, kept within children's sight but
out of their reach eg pushed to the back of
a deep shelf. Paper clips, split pins, safety
pins, elastic bands, double-sided sticky
tape, masking tape, blunt darning needles
and thread, hole punch, string, wool, wire,
nails (if provision for woodwork is
available), transparent covering film.

What to do

Keep in the drawers all small items
necessary for attaching surfaces together
when adhesive will not suffice. Stick one
item on the front of each drawer using
covering film. Ask the children for their
ideas about what they think would be best
to use. Because of the possibility of some
children putting paper clips, needles etc in
their mouths, tell the children that they
must ask a grown-up if they want to use
these items. Keeping these items visible but
out of reach ensures that children can still
have the opportunity to think of various
solutions to their 'fixing' problems, but
without any safety risk.

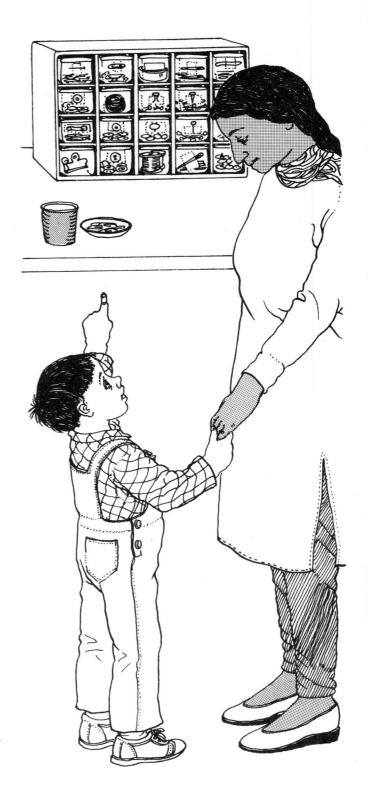

Art recipes

What you need
Powder paint; ice-cream cartons; old dessert spoons; paint thickeners eg powder adhesive, flour, washing powder, shaving cream etc; oil; water; card; felt-tipped pens.

What to do
The preparation of art media can provide valuable learning opportunities. Instead of preparing paint, adhesive, playdough etc away from the children, let them be involved. If the main paint store is situated outside the room, arrange to have in your 'art pantry' several ice-cream cartons of powder paint with lids. Normally, keep these out of the children's reach, but place them on the art table at the beginning of a paint mixing session with an adult. Give each child in the group a cottage cheese pot and let them choose a colour. Prepare a very simple 'recipe' chart and let each child mix a colour. Mixing paint, either with water only, or a wide variety of thickeners, such as powder adhesive, flour, soap flakes, shaving cream etc (for finger painting and printing) can involve reading, estimating, counting, predicting and descriptive skills (too runny, gooey etc). This can be developed into allowing children to mix different colours, and also, different shades of one colour, by adding varying amounts of white. Involve the children also in the mixing of adhesive (with powder adhesive, flour and water) and play dough. In all mixing activities with small groups encourage as much conversation as possible.

Tools of the trade

What you need

A wide variety of household items eg cotton buds, cotton wool, empty roll-on deodorant bottles, wire scouring pads, toothbrushes, corrugated cardboard, doilies; odd items of construction games eg old Lego; natural objects eg leaves, seeds, shells etc; food eg pasta, dried beans, coffee granules etc; Plasticine.

What to do

Through discussion, encourage the children to think about and suggest their own ideas for using items as art implements eg different items to apply paint, or to use as imprints on Plasticine for printing. Encourage the children to suggest the use of items from different interest areas eg shells from the discovery area for printing, or fir cones or a potato masher for Plasticine imprints. Stress that they must ask your permission before they take items from other areas into the art area. Encourage creative thinking by discussing the items in the art area, for example, 'collage' materials, with small groups.

The quiet area
Table-top activities

What you need
Jigsaws; mosaics; pegboards; card games; construction sets which are not suitable for floor play; beads, pasta, shells etc for threading; sewing resources.

What to do
Code all box lids, tidy drawers etc in their relevant colour. If you wish to limit the number of children playing with an item, write the maximum number of children on the front of the box lid, or side of container. Occasionally split the tables so that two children may sit together to share an item.

Support individual children as they play in this area by sometimes sitting next to them and trying out their ideas. Encourage co-operation by occasionally suggesting that the two children who are both making the same item may like to combine them to make one large building.

Some children may enjoy taking their play one stage further, (putting play people in the hospital, for example). Sometimes, it may be appropriate to ask what the 'machine' etc can be used for, or whether the child can think of a way to make it move (by adding string, or using a magnet etc). At other times, the child may decide simply to put the model on the display shelves to show others later. Much valuable pre-maths language (belongs to, bigger than, next to etc) can arise during conversations with individuals and groups in the quiet area.

The discovery area

Sand play

What you need
Two sand trays, with covers, one for wet sand, one for dry; one outdoor sand pit, if possible; graded sand buckets; spades; rakes; combs; potato masher; items for making imprints in wet sand; hollow bricks; plastic moulds and cutters; balance scales; shells; fir cones; stones; twigs; plastic cars; play people, animals, dinosaurs etc; small junk items; wide, flexible tubing.

What to do
Provide opportunities for both monitored individual play and small group activities. Encourage imaginative creations of 'sandscapes', especially in the larger outdoor sand pit. Allow children to use shells, cars, play people, twigs, animals etc to create 'gardens', race tracks, jungles, moonscapes, treasure hunts, tunnels and mines. Provide cardboard tubes or wide plastic tubing, down which children can put small play people. It is necessary to structure sandscape play to avoid the possibility of children putting too many toys in the sand, without the adults' knowledge. Place a selection of toys and plastic food cartons on a tray for the children to use.

Water play

What you need
One water trough (transparent if possible), one small plastic goldfish bowl or tank, transparent tubing, water toys, (water wheel etc), syphon, tea set, squeezy bottles, oil, food colouring, graded containers, plastic milk bottles, toy boats, submarines (commercially produced or home-made), play people, small plastic construction toys, shells, pebbles, stones, sand, seaweed, silver and coloured foil, brightly coloured Plasticine, fish-shape pastry cutters, white wool.

What to do
For demonstration purposes, it is interesting to make use of small plastic goldfish bowls or tanks which are clearly visible to small groups. Allow for fantasy 'underwater world' play. Let the children create underwater cities using Plasticine, sand, pebbles, Lego etc. Fish, octopuses, eels etc can be made from Plasticine suspended on the end of white wool. Play people can dive off toy boats and go hunting for Lego shipwrecks. Let the children experiment with Plasticine to find a boat shape which floats.

Discovery baskets

What you need
Plastic baskets each containing shells, seaweed, starfish etc; leaves, twigs, seeds, nuts, pebbles, stones; fossils, bones, teeth, claws, feathers; mirrors, magnifying glasses, colour paddles, magnets; baskets based on the five senses (eg musical instruments for 'listening', sets of articles in different shades of one colour for 'looking' etc); 'tinkering items' eg screws, nuts, bolts, cogs, levers, wheels, pulleys etc; broken bits of machinery (eg old clocks etc); balance scales (these could be kept also in the Maths area); card; felt-tipped pens.

What to do
Collect different baskets of natural and man-made objects for children to explore individually, in pairs and in groups. Through conversation, encourage the children to verbalise the discoveries they have made through their senses. Develop the children's skills of observing, describing and reasoning about what they see, hear, touch, taste and smell. Play 'guess what happened'. A child describes what he was playing with and others have to say what they think happened. For example, a child may say he put one magnet on top of the table and one underneath in the same place and.... Some children may also enjoy communicating their discoveries in the form of a painting, drawing or model. Based upon your observations of what children discover, make simple display labels.

Cooking

What you need
Table top cooker (out of children's reach), cooking equipment and ingredients, pictorial wall charts, aprons.

What to do
Cookery equipment may be kept either in the maths area or the discovery area. If a cooker is unavailable, there are many 'no cook' recipes, such as peppermint creams etc. As with paint mixing, encourage children to verbalise their discoveries. Ask what will happen if more water is added to the dough etc. Make very simple wall charts eg on handwashing, recipes etc. Send home copies of recipes to parents.

Living things

What you need
Hardy plants, carrot tops, growing seeds etc; mini-beasts, pets (permanent or on loan), card, felt-tipped pen.

What to do
Encourage the children to take responsibility for looking after plants and animals, and to co-operate with each other. Make simple charts about watering, feeding and cleaning requirements. Sometimes it may be possible to 'borrow' a pet for a day, to use for topic work.

Out-of-doors
An outdoor play space

What you need
Large items eg see-saws, slides, climbing frames, tunnels, logs etc; 'push n'pull' items eg carts, trains, bicycles etc, small apparatus eg bean bags, balls, skipping ropes, skittles, hoops etc.

What to do
Outdoor play can offer a child a great deal more than simply the chance to 'let off steam'. If adults can observe and involve themselves in children's outdoor play many opportunities for developing social (eg turn taking), imaginative (eg role play), intellectual (eg spatial awareness) and problem-solving skills can be developed. Watch and talk with the children as they play. If a fenced area just beyond the classroom door can be provided, let two children at a time out to play. Keep a basket of small apparatus handy by the door for the children to devise their own games eg throwing a beanbag into a hoop etc.

Improvised outdoor play equipment

What you need
Cardboard cartons, bucket, chalk, blankets, tables, carpet squares, theme area furniture, sand/water trays.

What to do
Use cardboard boxes to make large pretend walls, boats etc. Write numbers on a single box to make a large die. Chalk a number line on the ground. Get the children to throw the box die and jump along the line or carpet squares accordingly. In summer, throw blankets over classroom tables to make dens, and bring out theme area equipment and classroom sand and water trays. Devise aiming games (chalk a bullseye on a wall) such as throwing a beanbag in a bucket. In reception classes, it may be possible to use some of the indoor PE apparatus such as benches, jumping boxes etc for obstacle courses on a summer's day.

Settling in

Chapter three

Getting started

LEAs and individual playgroups, nurseries and schools adopt a wide variety of admission policies. These may include part-time attendance, going home for lunch and staggered entry. Whatever the arrangement the policies must be flexible to cater for individual needs.

Parents fulfil a very important role in settling children in a playgroup or nursery school (see page 75). It is a big step for parents to hand over responsibility for their children, perhaps for the first time. Pre-school staff should ensure that this transition time is a positive experience for all concerned.

If children start primary school below the statutory school age, provision should be made which is based on good nursery practice. There should be provision for part-time places, a nursery staffing ratio, adequate facilities and financial resources, and an appropriate play-based curriculum.

If such provision is made, then when the time comes to start 'big school', the transition is made much more easily. However, even when children have received relevant pre-school experiences, starting 'big school', whether on the same site or in a new building, can be daunting.

There are large noisy playgrounds to cope with, getting changed for PE and bustling lunch times etc. The reception teacher needs to observe carefully how her children are coping with these new experiences, and, based upon her observations, draw up strategies for helping them.

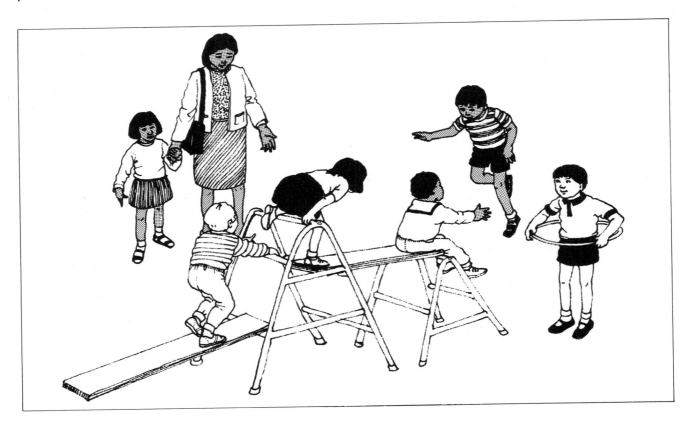

Looking around (P)

What you need
Plenty of adult helpers!

What to do
After reading the information booklet (see page 90) and talking with their child, parents will be ready to bring their child for some short visits.

The teacher, playgroup leader or adult helpers should make sure that the other children know the name of the visitor and they could discuss ways to make him feel at home. When showing the parent(s) and child round the nursery the teacher could take one or two older children with her to point out activities that they particularly enjoy.

Do not force the visiting child to join in with the group activities. He might feel happier observing from a distance until he feels more settled. After an initial visit together, parents could either stay with their child on a second visit, or, if he seems particularly confident, leave him for a short while. The number of visits will obviously vary from nursery to nursery but parents should feel that they can stay as long as necessary to settle their child into nursery or playgroup life.

A parent might promise to sit in a particular area, possibly preparing materials for collage, while the child tentatively begins to explore the room. As the child gains confidence over a few visits the parent might give a reason for popping out for a short time and return punctually. Eventually the child will want to stay for the full session.

Learning through talk

What you need
Cassette player, tapes.

What to do
Recent research (*Young Children Learning, Talking and Thinking at Home and School* by Professor B Tizard and M Hughes, Fontana Press) has revealed how much children develop intellectually through everyday extended conversations with adults at home. It is of tremendous benefit to children if similar opportunities for extended conversations with staff are made possible at pre-schools, particularly when staff have knowledge of children's home interests and activities. Arrange some meetings when you can discuss with parents ways in which you can share information about children's home experiences, so that these may be recognised and extended at pre-school, through conversation (see also 'Shared records', page 93).

The invitation (R)

What you need
A photograph of the teacher, photocopier.

What to do
Photocopy a head and shoulders photograph of yourself. Send a letter headed by the photograph to each child a week before their pre-school visit. Introduce yourself as their teacher, and explain some of the activities they will be doing on their visit.

Page Hill First School
Whitchurch
Herts.

Dear Kym
My name is Miss Bennet. I will be your teacher when you come to school after Easter. I am looking forward to meeting you next week when you can visit us and see some of the things you will be able to do at our school. I hope you will enjoy joining in our games and help us with our model making. You might like to bring one of your drawings to show us. See you soon!
from Miss Bennet

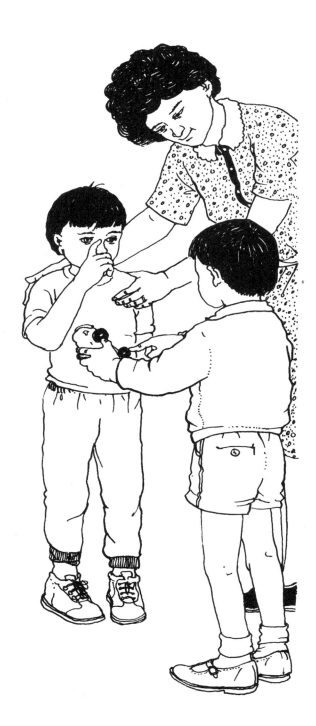

Visiting time (R)

What you need
Table toys, a surprise box, card, felt-tipped pens, crayons, sticky tape, string, extra adult helpers.

What to do
It is important that when the children enter the classroom for the first time, they should receive a positive impression. If the room looks like an Aladdin's cave most children will be so attracted by the options on offer that they will quite happily leave their parent's side. There is no need for parents to leave immediately. They might like to stay and play with the children for a while or to take the opportunity to become acquainted with some of the equipment.

To prevent any tears try the following suggestions:

- Have a wide variety of table toys including play dough, bead threading, simple jigsaws, tracing etc set out so the children may freely move from one to the other.
- Use the surprise box if you want to gather all the children together. They will soon forget all tears as they wait for the magic moment when the lid comes off and the surprise is revealed.
- Get the children busy making name labels. They can trace over their names and decorate the border with a pattern. The labels can be attached with sticky tape or string and the children can now be more easily identified.
- A really tearful child can sometimes be distracted by you or an adult helper drawing a happy face and a sad face, discussing all the features as she draws, and asking the child about his own face – is it happy or sad?

Comings and goings (R)

What you need

A separate entrance to the classroom eg a classroom back door, paper, felt-tipped pen.

What to do

If possible let parents bring their children straight into school via a separate school door. This will ensure that the new children do not get upset hanging around outside on a large crowded playground and are not overwhelmed by large numbers of older children.

Pre-plan the route for the new children and put up signs for the parents, directing them to a separate entrance. Parents can then help settle them into their first activity. Let the parents stay in the classroom until the children are happily absorbed in their first jigsaw, tracing etc. If a child is still tearful the surprise box brought out at this point will almost certainly attract the child's attention.

In the early days of term also have a separate picking up point for the parents to collect the reception children. You may want to use this time to go out for an informal chat with parents as well as in the morning.

Family album

What you need
A large photograph album, photographs of staff and helpers, felt-tipped pen, small pieces of paper.

What to do
Ask all adult staff or helpers to bring in a spare photograph of themselves to be made into an album for the library corner. Clearly label the photographs and use initially for discussion and later on for shared reading.

Play a recognition game by describing members of staff for the children to name. During the first couple of weeks ask the children to bring in recent photographs of themselves to be photocopied and put in the album.

Where does it come from?

What you need
The surprise box, one or two items from each interest area.

What to do
The children need to become familiar with the different interest areas and their contents. Turn the process into a game by using the surprise box. Reveal individual items from different interest areas. Ask questions about where the objects or games come from and discuss activities that can be done in each area. Also discuss the classroom posters, and the colour coding for each area.

Sardines

What you need
Interest area posters, specifying, by illustration and numerals, the number of children allowed in the area.

What to do
Deliberately send a large group of children into one of the interest areas. One child acts as the 'teacher' who calls out the names of the surplus children who then have to leave the area. The caller should calculate if he has left the correct number of children. This is one way of ensuring that the children realise exactly how many children are allowed in a particular area at one time.

Beat the egg-timer

What you need
Three egg-timers of one, three and five minutes, items from each interest area.

What to do
You will need to carefully introduce each interest area to one group of children at a time. Discuss the range of items in each area and their uses. Devise games to give practice in putting things away. For example, deliberately muddle up the tea set in the theme area and see if the children can beat the egg-timer in sorting it out and putting it away in the correct cupboards.

The conducted tour (R)

What you need
One or two older children.

What to do
On the first day at school, when everything is feeling very new and strange, the children can be taken on a conducted tour of the school introducing them to all the staff, dinner supervisors and any other helpers eg the school secretary and caretaker. The adults should be pre-warned about this visit so that they can provide a warm welcome for the children. A couple of older children could be taken along on this tour to answer the teacher's questions and provide personal opinions about school life.

Cloakroom rush hour

What you need
Numbered or illustrated name pegs.

What to do
Play some games at the beginning of 'outside time' or playtime to prevent all the children fetching their coats in one mad rush. Call out sets of children eg all those wearing blue shoes, to get their outdoor clothes first. An alternative would be to call out specific cloakroom peg numbers.

You could play this game with nursery or playgroup children by grouping the pictures on their pegs into sets eg 'All the children with a picture of a bird go and collect your coats'.

Up and over

What you need
The children's coats or jackets.

What to do
Teach the children in small groups, to lay out their coats or jackets in front of them on the floor with the coat open and the collar towards them. The children should put their arms in the holes and throw the coat over their head.

This method prevents the coat arms getting lost as the children struggle to put their coats on the conventional way and encourages greater independence in the cloakroom.

Let's play dinner supervisors (R)

What you need
Aprons, white headscarves, trays, pretend food, plastic plates, serving spoons, the school menu board.

What to do
Pre-school children are accustomed to having food placed in front of them whereas reception children often have to fetch the food themselves and make choices about what food to eat.

Get some of the children to act out the role of the dinner supervisors with you. The remaining children should study the school menu board, illustrated at first, practise lining up, and choose their dinner remembering to say 'please' and 'thank you'.

Let's pretend its lunchtime

What you need
Plasticine, wool cut up into small lengths, paper or plastic plates, plastic or real knives and forks, empty condiment sets and vinegar bottles.

What to do
Having a pretend lunchtime with the children can often eradicate many fears and inhibitions that they may have about food. Set out the table exactly like a lunchtime table with knives, forks and paper or plastic plates. Use empty salt, pepper and vinegar containers. Let the children practise cutting up the Plasticine food with the knives and forks. Sometimes use wool for spaghetti. By practising the actual physical movements involved in eating with a knife and fork and acting out the roles of children eating lunch they will be less apprehensive when it comes to midday.

Playtime blues (R)

What you need
A separate play area if possible adjoining the school playground, small PE equipment – if extra supervisors are available.

What to do
Pre-school children do not usually have any worries about going outside to play if this is done in relatively small groups with no older children around and using a small area of land. Reception children, however, are often frightened by the sheer size of a school playground and large numbers of older children milling around. Here are a few suggestions to prevent them being completely overwhelmed by playtime.

- Allow the children to play in a separate play area adjoining the main playground, or even in the area leading directly off the classroom, if possible, for the first few days.
- Stagger the break time so that the youngest children have separate playtime outside, supervised by their own teacher at first. Gradually integrate the children's play with other classes, just including one other class initially.
- Pair off children from older classes with the new children at playtimes and lunchtimes to minimise the trauma of life outside the sheltered classroom existence. Possibly introduce the pairs of children on the pre-school visit and arrange for the older ones to sit with the new children at lunchtime too.
- Let the children take small pieces of PE apparatus outside eg soft balls, bean bags, if extra supervisors are available. Chalk a target area on the playground wall to introduce an element of competition eg a numbered bullseye.
- If the playground does not have any

pre-painted games create your own by chalking number games eg hopscotch.

84

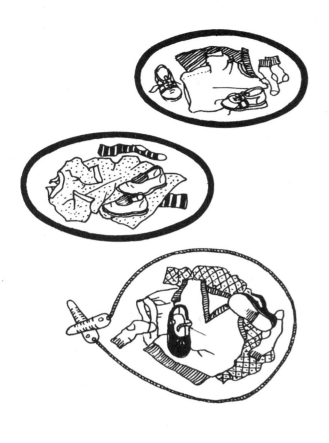

Where's my jumper? (R)

What you need
Large skipping hoops, skipping ropes.

What to do
Pre-school children are not used to getting themselves changed in large groups for PE and dance lessons. They often get muddled and young children can end up in tears looking for missing items of clothing. Here is a strategy to minimise the problems.

If space permits take the children to a large open space to get changed for PE or dance, preferably the side of the hall where they will be working. Put out well spaced hoops or skipping ropes shaped into a circle. Each child should place his clothes within the large hoop or rope circle. This way nothing gets lost and there is no dispute over ownership of unnamed items of clothing.

It's not fair – I had it first

What you need
A five minute egg-timer, a selection of toys.

What to do
Children playing together sometimes squabble over toys. Teaching children to say, 'Please can I have that toy after you' will not always work with every child, or will take time to develop. Another strategy you can adopt involves the use of a large egg-timer. Let each child play with the toy in question until the sand runs out and then pass it to the next child. The timer is then turned over and started again.

Taking turns

What you need
A tray of Unifix cubes in two colours, sorting hoops, a snap game, a long skipping rope, sequence strip jigsaw.

What to do
To help children learn the concepts of taking turns and co-operative play get them to do the following:
- Sorting the colours. Put the tray of Unifix cubes between two children. They have to take turns to sort each cube by colour into two hoops.
- Snap game.
- Skipping. Three children take turns to play 'higher and higher' with a skipping rope for jumping practice.
- Sequence jigsaw (R). Place the first pieces of the jigsaw in front of two children and divide the rest of the pieces equally between them. Get them to discuss what happens next and who owns the missing piece.

Keeping in touch

Chapter four

Parents in the picture

Parents are children's first teachers. A child will absorb information more rapidly during his first few years than at any other time in his life. Playgroup leaders, nursery and infant staff should take advantage of the special relationship between parent and child and continue to encourage parents in their valuable role as teachers.

It is important that parents are involved in their child's day-to-day education and share the aims and objectives of the staff. Parental involvement can be achieved by keeping parents informed at every stage and including parents in the record keeping process (see 'Shared records' on page 93). Regular communication minimises parental anxiety.

Many parents are keen to participate in their children's education and shared assignments. Whether they are in reading, maths or science they provide a good opportunity for parents to help their children learn. Children benefit from the regular contact between home and (pre) school and staff may learn information about the children's outside interests and capabilities that can be put to very good use in planning future activities.

Paving the way (P)

What you need
Slides of nursery children, projector, home-made video or large photographs of children, examples of nursery equipment.

What to do
Parents begin to worry about education when their children are still very young. This particularly applies if it is a first born child and the parents' only experience of nursery or playgroup is that of their own childhood. The parents need information but are sometimes unsure what questions to ask and what to look for in a good nursery or playgroup.

One way you can, as nursery or playgroup staff, reach out to parents is to visit local mother and toddler groups and give a talk. Equipment from the various interest areas could be shown and discussed and a slide or video show could be given demonstrating the development of a child's skills up to the time he starts school. Particular emphasis should be given to slides and photographs showing boys playing with traditionally girls' toys, eg dolls, and girls playing with traditionally boys' toys, eg train sets, Lego and construction toys.

You could recommend particular toys for the toddlers to be playing with at home, eg Duplo, thick crayons, small bricks, finger paints to develop fine motor control, dressing-up clothes, old hats, shoes etc for fantasy play and role modelling. You could also point out that two of the most valuable things a parent can be doing for their child at this stage is to talk to them and answer questions about everyday life, and look at books together.

Read all about it! (P)

What you need
Parents willing to type at home, spirit duplicator or photocopier, duplicating paper, stapler.

What to do
Once parents have tentatively chosen a nursery or playgroup it is useful for them to have a booklet containing all the information they need to know about daily routine and suggesting simple ways of preparing their children for a smooth, happy transition from home to playgroup or nursery. The brighter the booklet, the more likely it is that parents will take time to absorb fully the contents.

Include children's drawings to illustrate daily events. Clearly print the aims and objectives of the staff and give examples of ways to settle the children into the new environment with the minimum of upset eg let them wear clothes that are easy to get on and off with zips rather than buttons, elasticated trousers or skirts and slip on shoes.

Mention some of the play activities that will be going on and give some ideas to help parents foster the children's curiosity and investigative skills at home eg by sorting groceries, helping to make play dough, growing seeds on a window sill etc.

All parents are already involved in 'teaching' their children mathematical skills at home, be it setting the table, or sharing out sweets with a brother or sister but they do not always realise the learning potential of a situation.

The nursery or playgroup booklet can emphasise the value of such activities in developing the children's first mathematical concepts.

Home visits

What you need
A few toys, (pre) school information booklet.

What to do
In some areas parents and children can benefit by nursery or playgroup staff making a home visit to explain personally the aims of the nursery or playgroup. Introduce yourself to the family and demonstrate to the parents a few of the toys the child will be coming across. Shy children will soon lose their reserve if they have already met one of their teachers.

TYNEDALE PLAYGROUP
WEST STREET

DEAR PARENT,

YOU MAY BE AWARE THAT WE ARE ALWAYS IN NEED OF EXTRA HELPERS AT THE PLAYGROUP. IN FACT WE COULD NOT FUNCTION WITHOUT THE WILLING ROTA OF PARENT HELPERS. THERE ARE MANY AREAS WITHIN THE PLAY ENVIRONMENT HERE. YOU MAY FEEL YOU COULD OFFER SOME ASSISTANCE IN ONE OR MORE OF THEM. WE WOULD BE VERY GRATEFUL IF YOU COULD INDICATE BELOW ANY AREA THAT YOU WOULD BE WILLING TO HELP IN, GIVING TIMES AND DAYS CONVENIENT TO YOU.

WITH MANY THANKS, A.L.Brown

NAME:

READING TO THE CHILDREN

MIXING PAINTS + PAINTING SUPERVISION

CUTTING, STICKING, PATTERN MAKING

MODEL MAKING

SEWING AND COOKING

PLAYING GAMES

TALKING TO CHILDREN AT PLAY (A MOST IMPORTANT EXERCISE)

Can you help?

What you need
Duplicated forms, weekly notice.

What to do
Parents form an integral part of many playgroups, that could not exist without a willing rota of helpers. But some parents of nursery children are unsure how and if their help is needed. You need to make parents aware of the many areas in which their assistance will be gratefully received.

A form could be sent out listing the various ways parents can help eg: reading to children, helping with sticking and cutting, model-making and sewing, playing games, or talking to children as they play.

Playing with children is really one of the most important ways an adult can help develop children's powers of planning and logical thought.

What did they do today?

What you need
Refreshments – tea, coffee etc; card, felt-tipped pens.

What to do
Many working fathers and mothers do not get the opportunity to become involved in their children's nursery or playgroup education and have no idea what their children are doing during the day. By having an open evening to display some of the children's creative work and allowing both parents to take a closer look at group projects, parents can be encouraged to play a greater role in their children's educational, creative and social development.

For the open evening, you could label each set of pictures or models with the skills and concepts that are being developed in the child so that parents realise the importance of each sort of creative play.

Parents could also take the opportunity to have an informal discussion with you and other members of staff about their children's development. Working mothers in particular often feel rather left in the dark about their children's behaviour at nursery or playgroup as they tend to miss out on the everyday chatter and banter that develops between non-working mothers and playgroup or nursery staff.

Shared records

What you need
Shared record sheets.

What to do
Staff in playgroups, nurseries and reception classes are sometimes unaware of children's outside activities and achievements. Staff and helpers could be missing out on a wealth of learning activities based on the child's own interests. Regular communication between parents and staff is essential.

Have meetings with parents once or twice a term specifically for discussing their child's progress both in and out of nursery or school. Note down on the shared record sheets such interests as ballet, gymnastics or swimming and any special outings a child may have been on that you could follow up at (pre) school. Parents could point out various milestones that they notice their children achieving at home, eg when he first answers the telephone and relays a message or recognises a shop sign on a walk.

Read all about it (R)

What you need
Printed information booklets.

What to do
A few weeks before the start of term each set of parents should be given a printed booklet specifically about the reception class. They will probably already have received a school brochure. This booklet should include the following information:

- Photographs (photocopied if necessary) and names of all the staff and school personnel the reception child and his parents are liable to come into contact with in his first year at school. Parents and children could play memory games to learn the names.

- A plan of the infant school with hall, classrooms, playground, library and toilets clearly marked. Possibly a simple dice game could be printed for children to play with their parents, allowing them to become familiar with the various routes around the school. The first one in the reception classroom is the winner!

- Illustrations and short pieces of writing produced by older children describing enjoyable activities in school.

- Examples of letter and number formation with a reminder about using letter sounds rather than names.

- Information about the procedure for bringing children into school for the first couple of weeks.

- Do not worry statements! This section could be discussed with the children before they start school and will alleviate some of the common worries and fears experienced by many new reception children and their parents. For example:
Children will not be forced to eat food that they do not like.
Children can go to the toilet as often as

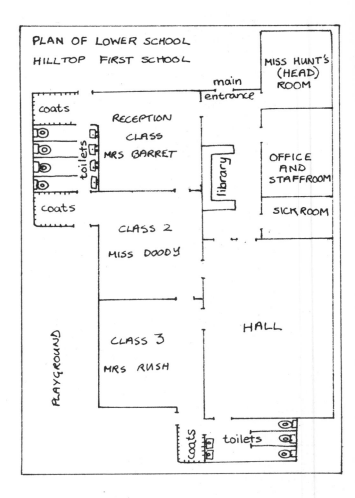

they need to and the teacher will not be cross if there is an 'accident'.
The children will not get lost going around the school – there will always be someone to show them the way.
The teacher does not expect them to be able to read and write before they start school!

At the end of the booklet there could be a short description of how parents can help in the classroom, with a tear-off form which can be returned to school.

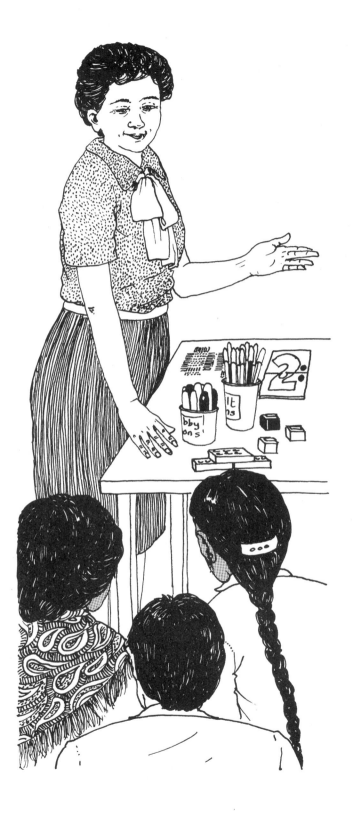

Up to big school – any questions?

What you need
Written invitations to parents, teacher or headteacher willing to give a talk.

What to do
Use one of the open evenings at nursery or playgroup for a talk given by a local headteacher or reception teacher and invite all the parents whose children will be going up to the infant school in the next three terms.

The speaker could stress that learning through play is just as important when children first start school as it has been in their nursery or playgroup education. Many parents are keen to teach their children the alphabet before they start school so it would be wise to discuss the fact that letter sounds rather than letter names should be taught, preferably within the context of fun games such as I Spy.

Other Scholastic books

Bright Ideas
The *Bright Ideas* books provide a wealth of resources for busy primary school teachers. There are now more than 20 titles published, providing clearly explained and illustrated ideas on topics ranging from *Word Games* and *Science* to *Display* and *Classroom Management*. Each book contains materials which can be photocopied for use in the classroom.

Teacher Handbooks
The *Teacher Handbooks* give an overview of the latest research in primary education, and show how it can be put into practice in the classroom. Covering all the core areas of the curriculum, the *Teacher Handbooks* are indispensable to the new teacher as a source of information and useful to the experienced teacher as a quick reference guide.

Management Books
The *Management Books* are designed to help teachers to organise their time, classroom and teaching more efficiently. The books deal with topical issues, such as *Parents and Schools* and organising and planning *Project Teaching,* and are written by authors with lots of practical advice and experiences to share.

Big Books
Big Books are poster-sized books, aimed at five- to nine-year-olds, which have been specially designed so that a group of children can share a book with an adult and still have that feeling of togetherness which is so important for early readers who are building up confidence. Included in each pack is a giant-sized book, six smaller books for individual reading and teacher notes.

Infant Science
Infant Science, written by teachers and advisers, introduces scientific concepts in non-fiction, easy-to-understand pupil books. Illustrated in full colour, the first books in the series on *Animals* show many aspects of living things from plants, insects and birds to fish and reptiles. A comprehensive teacher's guide giving practical activities and four A2 posters are also available.

Let's Investigate
Let's Investigate is an exciting range of photocopiable maths activity books giving open-ended investigative tasks. The series will complement and extend any existing maths programme. Designed to cover the six- to twelve-year-old age range these books are ideal for small group or individual work. Each book presents progressively more difficult concepts and many of the activities can be adapted for use throughout the primary school. Detailed teacher's notes outlining the objectives of each photocopiable sheet and suggesting follow-up activities have been included.

International Bookshelf
The *International Bookshelf* is a selection of informative educational books available in the UK exclusively through Scholastic. Truly representative of international thinking, these books are classics in their own field.